★ Superstar ★

SUDOKU

for Kids

ON THE GO

By Lindsay Small and Robin Hammond

PSS!
PRICE STERN SLOAN

PRICE STERN SLOAN
Published by the Penguin Group
Penguin Group (USA) Inc., 375 Hudson Street, New York, New York 10014, U.S.A.
Penguin Group (Canada), 90 Eglinton Avenue East, Suite 700,
Toronto, Ontario, Canada M4P 2Y3
(a division of Pearson Penguin Canada Inc.)
Penguin Books Ltd, 80 Strand, London WC2R ORL, England
Penguin Ireland, 25 St Stephen's Green, Dublin 2, Ireland
(a division of Penguin Books Ltd)
Penguin Group (Australia), 250 Camberwell Road, Camberwell, Victoria 3124, Australia
(a division of Pearson Australia Group Pty Ltd)
Penguin Books India Pvt Ltd, 11 Community Centre, Panchsheel Park,
New Delhi - 110 017, India
Penguin Group (NZ), Cnr Airborne and Rosedale Roads, Albany, Auckland 1310, New Zealand
(a division of Pearson New Zealand Ltd)
Penguin Books (South Africa) (Pty) Ltd, 24 Sturdee Avenue, Rosebank,
Johannesburg 2196, South Africa

Penguin Books Ltd, Registered Offices:
80 Strand, London WC2R ORL, England

ISBN 0-8431-2095-9   10 9 8 7 6 5 4 3 2 1

Contents

How to Do Sudoku Puzzles

Sudoku and Go!

The puzzles in this book are graded so that you can work your way through the levels and become a Sudoku superstar! Within each level, the puzzles get progressively harder. For example, the first 6x6 puzzle, puzzle 21, is the easiest, and the last 6x6 puzzle, puzzle 60, is the hardest. Remember that much of the joy of Sudoku is in the satisfaction of completing a puzzle. If you work at the right level, each puzzle will take you between 15 and 30 minutes.

After you've tried a few Sudoku puzzles, check out our special Sudoku Extra puzzles, which start on page 201! Not only do you solve the Sudoku puzzle itself, but you will uncover a hidden code word that will test your knowledge of the United States of America . . . a perfect way to keep you busy on long journeys!

So what are you waiting for? Get Sudokuing!

How to Sudoku

Although Sudoku puzzles are made up of numbers, there is no math involved. You must use logic to work out where the numbers go, and that is what makes the puzzles fun. Every puzzle is different, and once you get the hang of it, you may find yourself wanting to do more and more!

?	?	?	?
?	?	?	?
?	?	?	?
?	?	?	?

4x4 Sudoku Puzzles

Let's start with a nice easy puzzle made up of 4 mini-grids of 4 squares each. You will find these types of puzzles at the beginning of the book (puzzles 1–20). The aim of the puzzle is to place the numbers 1, 2, 3, and 4 in every column, row, and mini-grid.

1	2	4	3
3	4	2	1
2	3	1	4
4	1	3	2

Column

1	2	4	3
3	4	2	1
2	3	1	4
4	1	3	2

Row

1	2	4	3
3	4	2	1
2	3	1	4
4	1	3	2

Mini-grid

The trick is that in each column, row, and mini-grid the number can only be used once. There is only one way to finish each puzzle. But don't worry—if you think carefully, you will be able to work out the answer!

Step-by-Step Sudoku

Let's start by looking at the second column of the puzzle below. We already have the numbers 2 and 4 in that column, so we need to replace the A and B in the diagram with a 1 and a 3. We can't put a 3 in the top square because there is already a 3 in that row. So the A must be a 1 and the B must be a 3. That's a good start!

	A	3	
	2		
	B	1	
	4		

Now we need to work out what goes in the third column. Look at the diagram below. We need to replace the C and the D with a 2 and a 4. We can't put a 2 in the C-place because there is already a 2 in that row, so C must be 4. And we can't put a 4 in the D-place because there is already a 4 in that row, so D must be 2.

	1	3	
	2	C	
	3	1	
	4	D	

Remember that each mini-grid must have the numbers 1, 2, 3, and 4 in them, too. If we look at the second row of the diagram below we can see that we need a 1 and a 3. If we put a 3 where the G is, there would be two 3s in the top right mini-grid, which is not allowed. So the G must be a 1, and the F must be a 3. It is easy, then, to complete the two top mini-grids.

	1	3	E
F	2	4	G
	3	1	
	4	2	

Let's try the bottom left mini-grid now, which is missing a 1 and a 2. Looking along the rows, we see a 1 in the third row and a 2 in the fourth row. This tells us that H must be 2 and that J must be 1. Can you work out what K and L must be? Congratulations! You have done your first Sudoku!

4	1	3	2
3	2	4	1
H	3	1	K
J	4	2	L

6x6 Sudoku Puzzles

Now let's try a 6x6 puzzle, this time placing the numbers 1 to 6 in every column, row, and mini-grid. Remember that you can use each number only once! There are forty 6x6 puzzles in this book, puzzles 21–60, so you can have lots of practice!

In the puzzle below you can see that we need to place a 1, 2, and 5 in the first column in place of the A, B, and C. Look at the gray highlighted numbers. Can you figure out why the C can only be a 1? Once you fill in the 1, you can figure out that the B is a 2, because there is already a 5 in that row. What's left for the A? The 5! Simple, right?

A					6
B	3		5		4
C				5	2
3	5				
4		3		6	
6					

Triplet Trick

Look at the highlighted squares. In the top left mini-grid, the 5 is in the left column. In the middle left mini-grid, the 5 is in the middle column. In the bottom left mini-grid, the 5 MUST go in the right column. We call this method "working out triplets."

5					6
2	3		5		4
1				5	2
3	5				
4		3		6	
6					

Now look at the right-hand side of the puzzle. There is already a 5 in place in the top and middle mini-grids. Now you have to figure out where the 5 in the bottom mini-grid can go. Can you figure it out? Great! You've mastered the triplet trick!

5					6
2	3		5		4
1				5	2
3	5				
4		3		6	
6		5			

See if you can do the rest of the puzzle yourself. Here is a clue—start with the far right column!

5					6
2	3		5		4
1				5	2
3	5				
4		3		6	5
6		5			

9x9 Sudoku Puzzles

Puzzles 61–90 and most of the Sudoku Extra puzzles at the back of the book are 9x9 puzzles. They start easy and get harder and harder, so it is best to work carefully through the book and not begin with anything too difficult!

You might have guessed that, in a 9x9 Sudoku puzzle, each column, row, and mini-grid must contain the numbers 1 through 9. And you've probably guessed again that each number can be used only once.

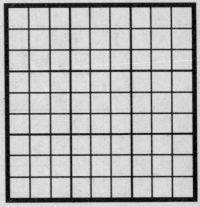

When you are doing the large Sudoku puzzles, it is helpful to start by searching for the triplets. Look at the highlighted 1s in the puzzle on the left. The bottom right mini-grid has only one square available for a 1. That's nice and easy!

15

Now look at the highlighted 8s. In the center mini-grid, the 8 must go in the middle row, in one of two positions. But if you look down you can see an 8 in the right square, which means that in the middle grid the 8 must go in the square on the left (marked X). Since this is the only possible square for the 8, it is safe to put it there.

Sometimes you don't know for certain which square to put a number in, and must look for more clues. Don't guess! You can find yourself in a big mess if you do! If you are not absolutely sure of a number, keep looking for more clues.

	5			1			9	
3		7	5		2	1		4
	6		4		3		5	
8		5				9		6
	3	2	x	6		4	7	
6		9				8		1
	8		2		1		4	
7		4	6		8	3	1	9
	1			4			8	

You might find it helpful to make notes by using a pencil to write small numbers into the grid. You can always erase the incorrect numbers later. Here's an example below. In this case, you know by looking at the triplet of 5s that one of these two highlighted boxes in the bottom left mini-grid must have a 5.

	5			1			9	
3		7	5		2	1		4
	6		4		3		5	
8		5				9		6
	3	2	8	6		4	7	
6		9				8		1
⁵8			2		1		4	
7		4	6		8	3	1	9
⁵1				4			8	

Another technique you can use is to look at a square and try to decide what numbers can go into it by eliminating the possibilities. Look at the highlighted square below. Now start counting to eliminate the possibilities: There is a 1 in the column, so a 1 is out. There are a 2, 3, and 4 in the row, so those numbers are out. A 5 is in the mini-grid and a 6 is in the column. A 7 is in the row. There is no 8, so that's a possibility. Look! There's a 9 in the column. So 8 is your number!

5			1			9	
3		7	5		2	1		4
	6		4	9	3		5	
8		5				9		6
	3	2	8	6		4	7	
6		9				8		1
	8		2		1		4	
7		4	6		8	3	1	9
	1			4			8	

Remember that all Sudoku puzzles are different, and don't be too frustrated if you get stuck on one. If you leave it for a while and come back to it later, you will probably see a clue that you missed earlier.

Now the time has come for you to be a Sudoku superstar!

18

Puzzle Number 1

Fill in the grid so that every column,
every row, and every 2x2 box contains
the digits 1 to 4.

		1	
4			
			3
	2		

Fill in the grid so that every column, every row, and every 2x2 box contains the digits 1 to 4.

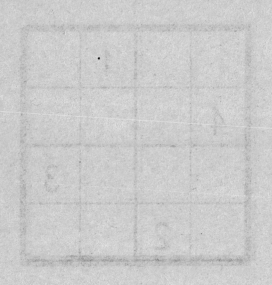

Puzzle Number 2

Fill in the grid so that every column,
every row, and every 2x2 box contains
the digits 1 to 4.

1		3	
	4		2

Puzzle Number 3

Fill in the grid so that every column, every row, and every 2x2 box contains the digits 1 to 4.

		3	
4			
			1
	1		

Fill in the grid so that every column, every row, and every 2x2 box contains the digits 1 to 4.

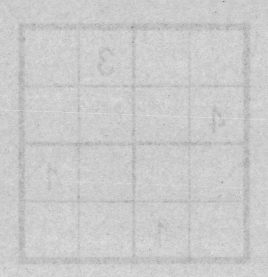

Puzzle Number 4

Fill in the grid so that every column, every row, and every 2x2 box contains the digits 1 to 4.

		3	4
2	3		

Puzzle Number 4

Fill in the grid so that every column,
every row and every 2x2 box contains
the digits 1 to 4.

Puzzle Number 5

Fill in the grid so that every column,
every row, and every 2x2 box contains
the digits 1 to 4.

4		3	
	2		3

Fill in the grid so that every column,
every row, and every 2×2 box contains
the digits 1 to 4.

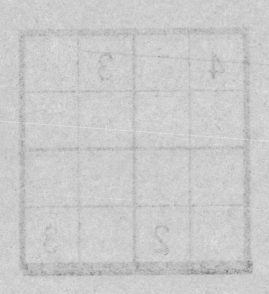

Puzzle Number 6

Fill in the grid so that every column,
every row, and every 2x2 box contains
the digits 1 to 4.

2		3	
	1		2

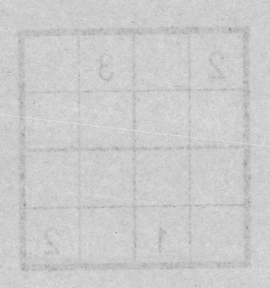

Puzzle Number 7

Fill in the grid so that every column,
every row, and every 2x2 box contains
the digits 1 to 4.

		4	
	1		
		3	
	2		

Puzzle Number 8

Fill in the grid so that every column, every row, and every 2x2 box contains the digits 1 to 4.

		4	
	3		
		1	
	2		

Fill in the grid so that every column, every row, and every 2x2 box contains the digits 1 to 4.

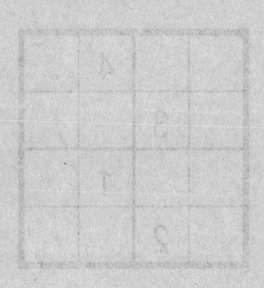

Puzzle Number 9

Fill in the grid so that every column, every row, and every 2x2 box contains the digits 1 to 4.

		2	
	4		
		3	
	1		

Fill in the grid so that every column,
every row, and every 2x2 box contains
the digits 1 to 4

Puzzle Number 10

Fill in the grid so that every column,
every row, and every 2x2 box contains
the digits 1 to 4.

		4	
4			
			2
	1		

Fill in the grid so that every column,
every row and every 2×2 box contains
the digits 1 to 4.

Puzzle Number 11

Fill in the grid so that every column, every row, and every 2x2 box contains the digits 1 to 4.

		1	
	3		
		4	
	4		

Puzzle Number 12

Fill in the grid so that every column, every row, and every 2x2 box contains the digits 1 to 4.

1		2	
	2		3

Puzzle Number 12

Fill in the grid so that every column,
every row, and every 2x2 box contains
the digits 1 to 4.

Puzzle Number 13

Fill in the grid so that every column,
every row, and every 2x2 box contains
the digits 1 to 4.

		2	
	3		
		1	
	2		

Puzzle Number 14

Fill in the grid so that every column, every row, and every 2x2 box contains the digits 1 to 4.

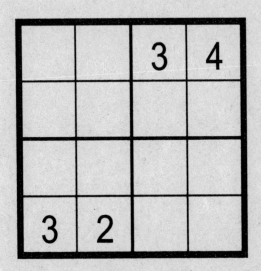

Fill in the grid so that every column,
every row, and every 2x2 box contains
the digits 1 to 4

Puzzle Number 15

Fill in the grid so that every column,
every row, and every 2x2 box contains
the digits 1 to 4.

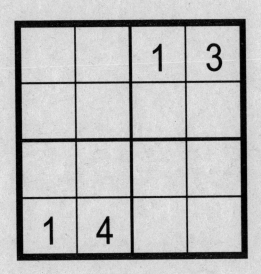

Puzzle Number 16

Fill in the grid so that every column,
every row, and every 2x2 box contains
the digits 1 to 4.

		3	
		4	
	3		
	1		

49

Fill in the grid so that every column, every row, and every 2x2 box contains the digits 1-4.

Puzzle Number 17

Fill in the grid so that every column, every row, and every 2x2 box contains the digits 1 to 4.

1		2	
	1		3

Fill in the grid so that every column, every row, and every 2×2 box contains the digits 1 to 4.

	2		1
3		1	

Puzzle Number 18

Fill in the grid so that every column, every row, and every 2x2 box contains the digits 1 to 4.

		1	
		2	
	1		
	3		

Puzzle Number 18

Fill in the grid so that every column,
every row, and every 2×2 box contains
the digits 1 to 4.

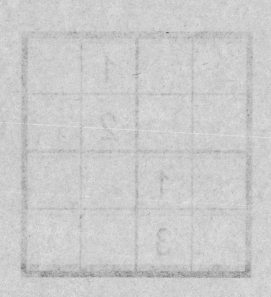

Puzzle Number 19

Fill in the grid so that every column, every row, and every 2x2 box contains the digits 1 to 4.

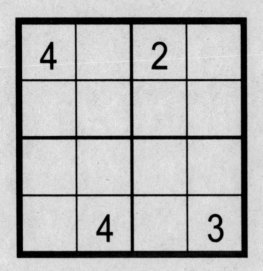

Fill in the grid so that every column, every row, and every 2x2 box contains the digits 1 to 4.

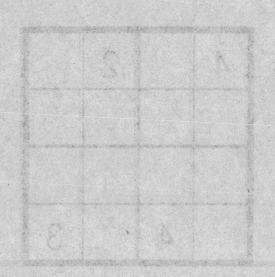

Puzzle Number 20

Fill in the grid so that every column,
every row, and every 2x2 box contains
the digits 1 to 4.

		4	
	4		
		1	
	3		

Puzzle Number 20

Fill in the grid so that every column, every row, and every 2x2 box contains the digits 1 to 4.

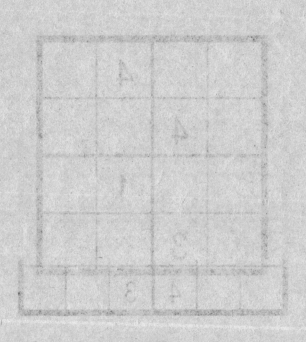

Puzzle Number 21

Fill in the grid so that every column,
every row, and every 3x2 box contains
the digits 1 to 6.

		1	5		
2					3
	6			1	
	4			3	
3					2
		4	3		

59

Puzzle Number 21

Fill in the grid so that every column, every row, and every 3x2 box contain the digits 1 to 6

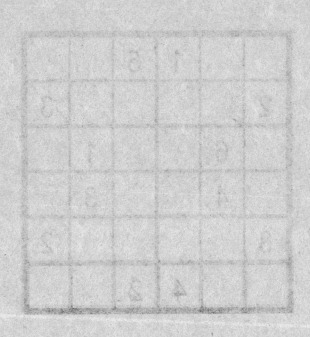

Puzzle Number 22

Fill in the grid so that every column,
every row, and every 3x2 box contains
the digits 1 to 6.

		5	6		
1					4
	6			3	
	2			6	
6					1
		4	2		

Puzzle Number 23

Fill in the grid so that every column,
every row, and every 3x2 box contains
the digits 1 to 6.

3					4
	2			6	
		5	6		
		4	3		
	4			3	
1					2

63

Puzzle Number 24

Fill in the grid so that every column,
every row, and every 3x2 box contains
the digits 1 to 6.

6					5
		4	6		
	3			5	
	1			4	
		3	5		
1					2

Fill in the grid so that every column,
every row and every 3x2 box contains
the digits 1 to 6

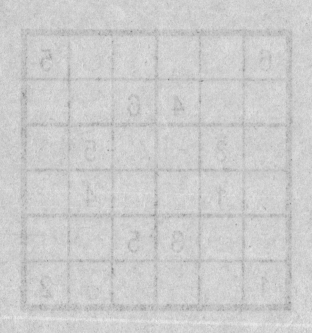

Puzzle Number 25

Fill in the grid so that every column, every row, and every 3x2 box contains the digits 1 to 6.

	6			1	
		3	2		
5					6
4					2
		1	3		
	2			5	

Fill in the grid so that every column,
every row and every 3×2 box contains
the digits 1 to 6.

Puzzle Number 26

Fill in the grid so that every column,
every row, and every 3x2 box contains
the digits 1 to 6.

		6	1		
5					4
	1			5	
	5			3	
3					6
		2	5		

69

Puzzle Number 27

Fill in the grid so that every column, every row, and every 3x2 box contains the digits 1 to 6.

	6			1	
5					2
		4	2		
		6	3		
3					5
	2			3	

Puzzle Number 28

Fill in the grid so that every column,
every row, and every 3x2 box contains
the digits 1 to 6.

		4	5		
	6			2	
5					2
1					4
	3			4	
		2	3		

Fill in the grid so that every column,
every row and every 2x3 box contains
the digits 1 to 6.

Puzzle Number 29

Fill in the grid so that every column,
every row, and every 3x2 box contains
the digits 1 to 6.

		2	1		
		6	4		
2					5
3					6
		3	6		
		4	5		

Fill in the grid so that every column,
every row and every 3×2 box contains
the digits 1 to 6

Puzzle Number 30

Fill in the grid so that every column,
every row, and every 3x2 box contains
the digits 1 to 6.

	5	1	4	2	
3					5
1					2
	3	2	1	5	

Puzzle Number 31

Fill in the grid so that every column, every row, and every 3x2 box contains the digits 1 to 6.

	3	4	2	5	
	5			3	
	6			4	
	2	3	4	1	

Puzzle Number 32

Fill in the grid so that every column, every row, and every 3x2 box contains the digits 1 to 6.

4					6
	3			2	
		1	6		
		6	5		
	2			6	
5					3

Fill in the grid so that every column,
every row, and every 3x3 box contains
the digits 1 to 9.

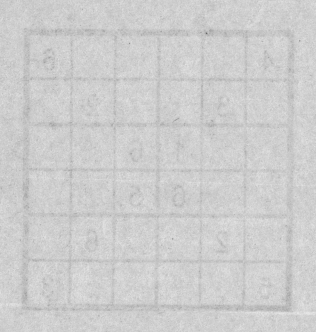

Puzzle Number 33

Fill in the grid so that every column,
every row, and every 3x2 box contains
the digits 1 to 6.

	5			2	
	6			1	
		3	4		
		6	5		
	2			4	
	3			5	

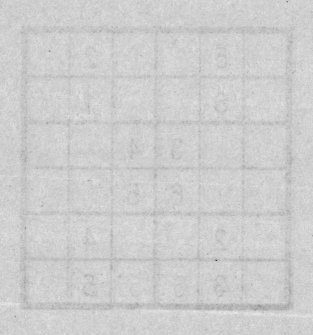

Puzzle Number 34

Fill in the grid so that every column, every row, and every 3x2 box contains the digits 1 to 6.

	3	2	1	6	
		1	6		
		5	4		
	4	6	5	3	

Puzzle Number 35

Fill in the grid so that every column,
every row, and every 3x2 box contains
the digits 1 to 6.

4					3
		2	6		
	2			5	
	3			6	
		1	2		
2					4

Puzzle Number 38

Fill in the grid so that every column,
every row, and every 3x2 box contains
the numerals 1 to 6.

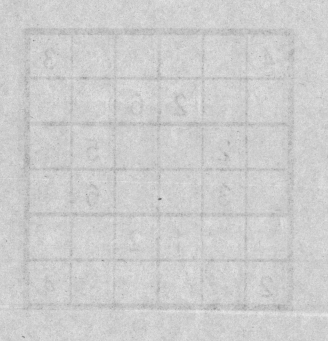

Puzzle Number 36

Fill in the grid so that every column, every row, and every 3x2 box contains the digits 1 to 6.

2		6	4		3
1					6
5					2
3		2	5		4

Fill in the grid so that every column, every row, and every 5x5 box contains the digits 1 to 5.

Puzzle Number 37

Fill in the grid so that every column, every row, and every 3x2 box contains the digits 1 to 6.

	3	1	5	4	
6					1
3					2
	4	3	6	2	

Fill in the grid so that every column, every row, and every 3x2 box contains the digits 1 to 6.

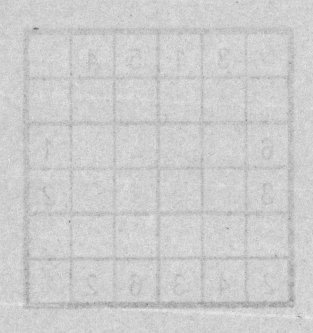

Puzzle Number 38

Fill in the grid so that every column,
every row, and every 3x2 box contains
the digits 1 to 6.

6					3
	4			5	
		3	2		
		2	4		
	1			2	
2					4

Puzzle Number 38

Fill in the grid so that every column,
every row and every 3x2 box contains
the digits 1 to 6

Puzzle Number 39

Fill in the grid so that every column, every row, and every 3x2 box contains the digits 1 to 6.

2					6
	3			5	
		1	6		
		4	3		
	1			6	
6					1

Puzzle Number 40

Fill in the grid so that every column, every row, and every 3x2 box contains the digits 1 to 6.

6		5	2		4
		4	6		
		3	1		
2		6	3		1

Fill in the grid so that every column, every row, and every 3x2 box contains the digits 1 to 6

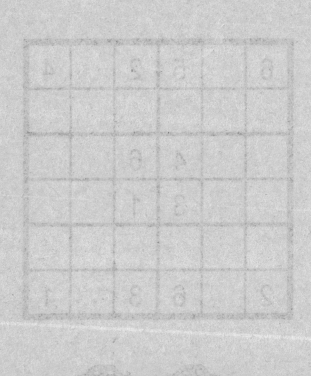

Puzzle Number 41

Fill in the grid so that every column, every row, and every 3x2 box contains the digits 1 to 6.

2		4	5		6
	5			1	
	2			6	
6		5	4		1

Puzzle Number 42

Fill in the grid so that every column,
every row, and every 3x2 box contains
the digits 1 to 6.

		2	4		
	3			5	
1					3
2					4
	1			6	
		6	1		

101

Puzzle Number 42

Fill in the grid so that every column,
every row, and every 3x2 box contains
the digits 1 to 6.

Puzzle Number 43

Fill in the grid so that every column, every row, and every 3x2 box contains the digits 1 to 6.

2	5			1	4
6					5
3					1
5	4			3	2

Fill in the grid so that every column,
every row, and every 3x2 box contains
the digits 1 to 6.

Puzzle Number 44

Fill in the grid so that every column,
every row, and every 3x2 box contains
the digits 1 to 6.

		6	3		
2					6
	1			2	
	6			5	
3					1
		1	2		

Puzzle Number 45

Fill in the grid so that every column,
every row, and every 3x2 box contains
the digits 1 to 6.

5					3
		1	6		
	1			3	
	2			6	
		4	2		
1					4

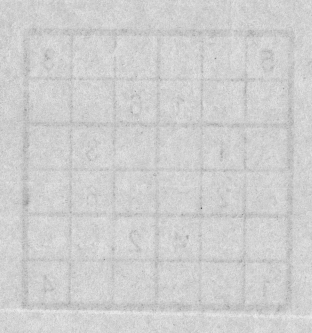

Puzzle Number 46

Fill in the grid so that every column, every row, and every 3x2 box contains the digits 1 to 6.

3					5
	2			4	
		2	6		
		3	4		
	1			3	
2					1

Fill in the grid so that every column, every row and every 3x2 box contains the digits 1 to 6

Puzzle Number 47

Fill in the grid so that every column,
every row, and every 3x2 box contains
the digits 1 to 6.

	3			6	
		6	4		
5					3
6					4
		5	1		
	1			5	

Puzzle Number 48

Fill in the grid so that every column,
every row, and every 3x2 box contains
the digits 1 to 6.

	4			1	
	6			2	
6					2
4					3
	3			6	
	1			3	

Fill in the grid so that every column,
every row, and every 3x2 box contains
the digits 1 to 6.

Puzzle Number 49

Fill in the grid so that every column, every row, and every 3x2 box contains the digits 1 to 6.

	5	4	2	6	
	1			2	
	3			4	
	4	2	5	3	

Puzzle Number 50

Fill in the grid so that every column, every row, and every 3x2 box contains the digits 1 to 6.

1					2
3					6
	1			2	
	5			6	
5					3
4					5

117

Puzzle Number 59

Fill in the grid so that every column,
every row and every 3x2 box contains
the digits 1 to 6

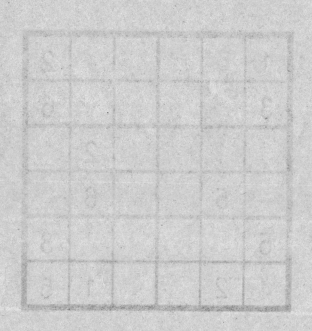

Puzzle Number 51

Fill in the grid so that every column,
every row, and every 3x2 box contains
the digits 1 to 6.

	6			3	
3					6
		3	4		
		2	3		
5					2
	2			1	

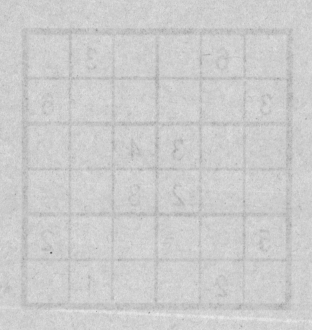

Puzzle Number 52

Fill in the grid so that every column,
every row, and every 3x2 box contains
the digits 1 to 6.

6	5			1	4
5					2
3					1
4	1			5	3

121

Puzzle Number 52

Fill in the grid so that every column,
every row, and every 3x2 box contains
the digits 1 to 6.

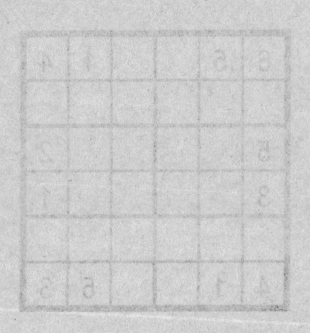

Puzzle Number 53

Fill in the grid so that every column,
every row, and every 3x2 box contains
the digits 1 to 6.

	6			5	
		5	2		
4					3
6					5
		6	1		
	1			6	

Puzzle Number 54

Fill in the grid so that every column, every row, and every 3x2 box contains the digits 1 to 6.

5					1
	3			6	
	2			4	
	1			2	
	4			5	
2					3

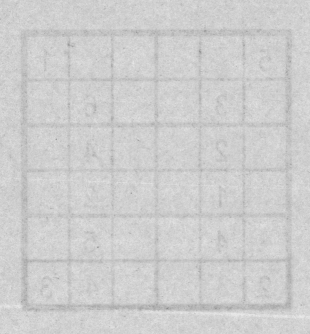

Puzzle Number 55

Fill in the grid so that every column,
every row, and every 3x2 box contains
the digits 1 to 6.

	1			5	
5					2
		1	5		
		3	4		
4					3
	3			4	

Puzzle Number 56

Fill in the grid so that every column,
every row, and every 3x2 box contains
the digits 1 to 6.

4	3			1	6
6					2
2					4
5	2			4	3

Fill in the grid so that every column,
every row, and every 3x2 box contains
the digits 1 to 6.

Puzzle Number 57

Fill in the grid so that every column, every row, and every 3x2 box contains the digits 1 to 6.

5					3
		3	1		
		2	3		
		5	6		
		6	2		
1					6

131

Puzzle Number 58

Fill in the grid so that every column, every row, and every 3x2 box contains the digits 1 to 6.

2	4			5	3
1					4
6					2
4	6			2	1

- Fill in the grid so that every column, every row, and every 4×4 box contains the digits 1 to 6

Puzzle Number 59

Fill in the grid so that every column,
every row, and every 3x2 box contains
the digits 1 to 6.

2					5
		6	3		
	2			5	
	6			3	
		2	4		
6					2

Puzzle Number 60

Fill in the grid so that every column,
every row, and every 3x2 box contains
the digits 1 to 6.

3					5
6					2
		3	2		
		2	5		
1					3
2					1

Puzzle Number 61

Fill in the grid so that every column, every row, and every 3x3 box contains the digits 1 to 9.

	6		7	8	3		1	
4	7			6			5	8
		8				9		
		3	4		6	1		
9				5				4
		5	9			1	8	
		4				2		
2	5			9			4	1
	8		2	4	7		6	

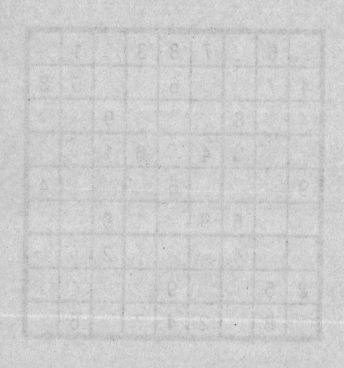

Puzzle Number 62

Fill in the grid so that every column, every row, and every 3x3 box contains the digits 1 to 9.

1	3			8			6	4
7		5	1	4	9	8		2
	8						1	
		8		9		4		
4	2						9	1
		1		2		5		
	5						4	
6		2	8	3	7	1		9
9	1			6			7	8

Fill in the grid so that every column,
every row, and every 3x3 box contains
the digits 1 to 9

Puzzle Number 63

Fill in the grid so that every column, every row, and every 3x3 box contains the digits 1 to 9.

4								6
3			8	1	7			9
9	1	7				3	8	5
			6	3	1			
2	3		4		8		9	1
			9	5	2			
8	4	9				2	1	3
5			1	8	4			7
6								8

143

Puzzle Number 64

Fill in the grid so that every column,
every row, and every 3x3 box contains
the digits 1 to 9.

9		7	4		2	6		5
8			1		7			2
3			5		9			1
6	8						2	7
		2				4		
7	4						8	9
4			6		5			3
2			9		3			8
5		3	8		1	7		4

145

Puzzle Number 65

Fill in the grid so that every column,
every row, and every 3x3 box contains
the digits 1 to 9.

3								1
		2		4		3		
	7	1	5		6	4	8	
	3	4	2		7	6	5	
	6		4		3		9	
	5	9	6		1	2	3	
	9	3	8		2	5	1	
		7		6		8		
8								9

Puzzle Number 66

Fill in the grid so that every column,
every row, and every 3x3 box contains
the digits 1 to 9.

		1				5		
3			1		7			9
8			3	6	4			2
	6		7		5		9	
	3	8	9		1	4	7	
	4		8		6		2	
4			5	8	2			7
9			4		3			1
		7				3		

149

Fill in the grid so that every column, every row, and every marked 3x3 box contains the digits 1 to 9.

Puzzle Number 67

Fill in the grid so that every column,
every row, and every 3x3 box contains
the digits 1 to 9.

7								4
	9		7	8	6		2	
	3	5				6	7	
2	7		4		1		9	6
6				7				3
1	5		3		8		4	7
	6	2				4	3	
	4		6	9	2		1	
9								2

Fill in the grid so that every column, every row, and every 3x3 box contains the digits 1 to 9.

Puzzle Number 68

Fill in the grid so that every column,
every row, and every 3x3 box contains
the digits 1 to 9.

	2		4		3		1	
1		7	6		2	5		3
4								8
9	5			7			3	1
	7			4			6	
8	1			2			5	4
6								2
7		9	2			1	4	6
	8			7		4		9

153

Puzzle Number 69

Fill in the grid so that every column,
every row, and every 3x3 box contains
the digits 1 to 9.

	9		6		1		7	
1	8						6	2
6			5		2			1
2	6		4		8		3	5
		1				9		
8	4		3		5		2	7
7			2		9			4
4	3						5	9
	2		8		3		1	

155

Puzzle Number 70

Fill in the grid so that every column, every row, and every 3x3 box contains the digits 1 to 9.

	2		7	1	8		4	
5								3
	1		3	9	5		7	
		1				6		
4	3	7	1	6	2	5	9	8
		5				7		
	4		5	3	6		1	
9								2
	5		2	4	9		6	

Puzzle Number 71

Fill in the grid so that every column, every row, and every 3x3 box contains the digits 1 to 9.

	4						2	
1	5			2			3	8
6	2		4	8	7		5	9
			9	6	4			
	1		7		8		9	
			2	5	1			
8	9		5	4	6		1	7
4	7			9			8	2
	3						6	

159

Puzzle Number 72

Fill in the grid so that every column, every row, and every 3x3 box contains the digits 1 to 9.

		2	9	6	7	5		
4	5						9	6
	9	3				7	2	
	7		5		6		4	
		8	2		9	6		
	2		7		3		8	
	3	1				8	7	
2	6						1	9
		4	1	9	5	3		

161

Fill in the grid so that every column,
every row, and every 3x3 box contains
the digits 1 to 9.

Puzzle Number 73

Fill in the grid so that every column,
every row, and every 3x3 box contains
the digits 1 to 9.

	3		2		4		7	
7			8		3			6
	8		5	7	1		4	
		1		8		2		
	7	2	6		9	1	3	
		8		2		7		
	5		4	1	6		8	
4			9		8			7
	6		7		2		5	

Puzzle Number 74

Fill in the grid so that every column,
every row, and every 3x3 box contains
the digits 1 to 9.

		7		3		9		
1								5
2		5	1	9	8	7		6
7		2		4		3		8
8			2		3			1
3		6		5		2		7
4		3	5	1	2	8		9
9								4
		1		8		6		

165

Puzzle Number 75

Fill in the grid so that every column,
every row, and every 3x3 box contains
the digits 1 to 9.

	2	5	1		4	9	7	
3			5	7	2			1
1								2
	6			1			9	
	4		3	9	7		1	
	8			5			4	
8								4
2			7	4	1			9
	3	9	6		5	1	2	

167

Puzzle Number 76

Fill in the grid so that every column, every row, and every 3x3 box contains the digits 1 to 9.

	9	6	8		3	5	2	
5			9		2			4
		3		4		9		
	2			6			1	
3	8		7		9		6	2
	4			8			5	
		7		9		2		
9			1		5			6
	6	2	4		7	1	9	

Puzzle Number 77

Fill in the grid so that every column, every row, and every 3x3 box contains the digits 1 to 9.

	6	9		1		3	8	
			3		4			
	3		6	9	8		1	
5	9			7			4	1
6			5		2			8
4	8			6			7	5
	5		2	8	1		9	
			9		7			
	2	8		3		1	5	

Puzzle Number 78

Fill in the grid so that every column,
every row, and every 3x3 box contains
the digits 1 to 9.

		7	5	3	6	4		
	3		4	8	9		7	
6	5			2			3	8
9								7
		3		7		8		
7								5
1	4			5			9	3
	2		1	6	3		8	
		8	2	9	4	6		

173

Puzzle Number 79

Fill in the grid so that every column, every row, and every 3x3 box contains the digits 1 to 9.

	8		3	5	2		7	
	7			8			6	
		4		1		3		
	3	2	8		1	6	5	
8		9				1		7
	5	7	2		6	8	3	
		8		6		9		
	1			2			4	
	9		1	4	5		8	

Puzzle Number 80

Fill in the grid so that every column,
every row, and every 3x3 box contains
the digits 1 to 9.

6				8				9
5		9				2		1
	4	8				6	3	
	6		7	5	2		9	
	5	4	9		8	1	2	
	2		3	1	4		5	
	1	6				9	7	
7		3				5		8
4				7				2

Fill in the grid so that every column, every row, and every box contains the digits 1 to 9.

Puzzle Number 81

Fill in the grid so that every column, every row, and every 3x3 box contains the digits 1 to 9.

		7	4		1	5		
		9				1		
	1	3				8	6	
1	6		3		5		9	2
		4	1	9	2	6		
5	9		7		6		4	1
	8	6				2	1	
		5				9		
		1	2		7	4		

Puzzle Number 82

Fill in the grid so that every column,
every row, and every 3x3 box contains
the digits 1 to 9.

		9	4		1	3		
	4		6		5		7	
			7	2	3			
8	7			5			6	4
9		6		4		7		3
1	2			7			9	8
			8	1	2			
	3		5		7		8	
		5	9		4	6		

Fill in the grid so that every column,
every row, and every 3x3 box contains
the digits 1 to 9.

Puzzle Number 83

Fill in the grid so that every column, every row, and every 3x3 box contains the digits 1 to 9.

		4				7		
1	8						9	5
2		6	9		7	4		1
8		3	2		4	1		9
			1		6			
7		9	8		5	2		4
3		2	7		9	6		8
6	7						4	3
		8				5		

183

Puzzle Number 84

Fill in the grid so that every column,
every row, and every 3x3 box contains
the digits 1 to 9.

6	4		7	8	1		3	2
		8		5		7		
1			2		3			8
			9		8			
8	3	6				2	5	9
			6		5			
5			8		2			6
		1		7		9		
7	8		3	6	9		2	5

Puzzle Number 85

Fill in the grid so that every column, every row, and every 3x3 box contains the digits 1 to 9.

8	4			6			3	1
	3		9		8		7	
6			1		3			4
		3		7		5		
5	9	7				4	1	6
		8		9		3		
3			6		9			8
	8		2		7		6	
7	1			8			5	2

Puzzle Number 86

Fill in the grid so that every column, every row, and every 3x3 box contains the digits 1 to 9.

5		7	4	9	3	2		8
	8	2		1		3	4	
		4				9		
7			2		5			1
			3		9			
4			1		8			9
		9				7		
	4	1		3		5	6	
2		6	5	8	4	1		3

Puzzle Number 87

Fill in the grid so that every column,
every row, and every 3x3 box contains
the digits 1 to 9.

4			3		1			9
	6		2		4		3	
3		5		9		4		2
	9	1				7	4	
		3	7		9	5		
	5	8				9	6	
1		7		2		3		4
	3		1		7		9	
9			5		3			7

Puzzle Number 88

Fill in the grid so that every column, every row, and every 3x3 box contains the digits 1 to 9.

2				5				1
		8				3		
	3		9	7	1		2	
8	9	6				2	1	3
5	2						4	6
3	7	4				5	8	9
	8		7	1	2		9	
		9				8		
7				9				4

Puzzle Number 89

Fill in the grid so that every column, every row, and every 3x3 box contains the digits 1 to 9.

		7	8		4	2		
	2	9		7		1	5	
4	3			1			8	7
		3		2		7		
	9		7		5		4	
		6		4		9		
3	6			9			7	1
	7	1		8		5	9	
		4	1		7	8		

195

Puzzle Number 90

Fill in the grid so that every column, every row, and every 3x3 box contains the digits 1 to 9.

			5	1	4			
	2		9	7	6		8	
	4	7				5	6	
6	8		1		3		4	7
				9				
7	1		4		2		5	9
	3	4				6	9	
	7		3	4	9		2	
			6	2	5			

197

Sudoku Extra 91

When you have completed this Sudoku puzzle, use the
code box to work out the secret, highlighted word.
(You may not need to use all the letters.)

		6	2		
	1			3	
5					3
3					4
	2			5	
		3	6		

1	2	3	4	5	6
N	I	L	E	A	M

Clue
This state is also known as the Pine Tree State,
with nearly 90 percent of the land covered
in forests!

Sudoku Extra 92

When you have completed this Sudoku puzzle, use the code box to work out the secret, highlighted word. (You may not need to use all the letters.)

	2			3	
		3	4		
6					1
5					6
		4	6		
	6			1	

1	2	3	4	5	6
A	P	O	W	I	R

Clue
Farms make up about 89 percent of this state's land, and it raises more hogs than anywhere else in the world! Do you know what it is?

Sudoku Extra 93

When you have completed this Sudoku puzzle, use the
code box to work out the secret, highlighted word.
(You may not need to use all the letters.)

	1	6	2	5	
6					3
4					2
	4	5	6	3	

1	2	3	4	5	6
U	E	A	H	R	T

Clue
The seagull is this state's official bird, and the
sego lily is its official flower.

203

Sudoku Extra 94

When you have completed this Sudoku puzzle, use the code box to work out the secret, highlighted word. (You may not need to use all the letters.)

	5			4	
		1	5		
4					2
6					3
		4	3		
	6			2	

1	2	3	4	5	6
E	V	A	A	D	N

Clue
Also known as the Silver State, this state's capital is Carson City.

205

Sudoku Extra 95

When you have completed this Sudoku puzzle, use the
code box to work out the secret, highlighted word.
(You may not need to use all the letters.)

4					2
		5	4		
		6	3		
		1	6		
		4	2		
1					6

1	2	3	4	5	6
E	X	V	A	S	T

Clue
The Lone Star State is famous for its
farms and ranches, but it also has over
six hundred miles of beaches!

Sudoku Extra 96

When you have completed this Sudoku puzzle, use the code box to work out the secret, highlighted word. (You may not need to use all the letters.)

5			8		6			1
	3			9			4	
		4	3	2	7	9		
7	2						3	8
		5	2		8	6		
9	8						1	2
		9	5	6	1	2		
	6			3			9	
1			9		2			4

1	2	3	4	5	6	7	8	9
C	I	R	O	M	U	S	S	I

Clue:
Fifty-five hundred caves have been discovered in this state, which is where Walt Disney spent much of his childhood.

Sudoku Extra 97

When you have completed this Sudoku puzzle, use the code box to work out the secret, highlighted word. (You may not need to use all the letters.)

		7		5		3		
	4			1			2	
8			4		6			5
7	3		5		8		1	6
		9				2		
2	8		9		3		4	7
1			6		9			3
	5			4			9	
		6		3		7		

1	2	3	4	5	6	7	8	9
G	I	E	O	G	G	O	A	R

Clue:
Also known as the Peach State, this state's capital is Atlanta.

Sudoku Extra 98

When you have completed this Sudoku puzzle, use the code box to work out the secret, highlighted word. (You may not need to use all the letters.)

9	6						5	8
	2		6	5	9		1	
		5				4		
		3	2		7	1		
	8	2	4		5	6	3	
		4	9		6	8		
		9				7		
	4		7	9	1		8	
5	1						2	4

1	2	3	4	5	6	7	8	9
P	A	L	O	R	Y	M	I	E

Clue:
Did you know that Washington is the only state named for a president? This is its capital.

Sudoku Extra 99

When you have completed this Sudoku puzzle, use the code box to work out the secret, highlighted word. (You may not need to use all the letters.)

	8	1	5	3	2	6	4	
4								2
		6		4				
	6		1	8	3		7	
9	4						2	8
	7		4	2	9		5	
		9		6				
2								5
	3	4	2	5	1	8	9	

1	2	3	4	5	6	7	8	9
W	R	A	E	E	D	L	T	A

Clue:
This state was the first to ratify the Constitution of the United States, which is how it got its nickname, the First State.

Sudoku Extra 100

When you have completed this Sudoku puzzle, use the code box to work out the secret, highlighted word. (You may not need to use all the letters.)

3	4						8	6
5	7			9			4	1
		6				5		
9			4		8			2
	1	2	9		6	4	5	
6			7		2			8
		3				7		
7	2			6			3	9
4	8						6	5

1	2	3	4	5	6	7	8	9
C	K	D	A	E	I	C	H	E

Clue:
This is the state bird of Massachusetts, famous for such historical events as the Boston Massacre and the Boston Tea Party, as well as the midnight ride of Paul Revere.

Sudoku Extra 101

When you have completed this Sudoku puzzle, use the code box to work out the secret, highlighted word. (You may not need to use all the letters.)

9			5	3	2			7
	5	6		4		2	1	
	7			9			3	
	6						7	
		7	9	8	1	5		
	8						2	
	4			6			9	
	3	1		7		8	5	
2			8	1	3			6

1	2	3	4	5	6	7	8	9
D	A	R	I	L	E	F	O	F

Clue:
This state is known as the Sunshine State, or sometimes the Peninsula State, because it gets sunshine all year long and juts four hundred miles out into the ocean!

219

Sudoku Extra 102

When you have completed this Sudoku puzzle, use the code box to work out the secret, highlighted word. (You may not need to use all the letters.)

		7		9		8		
8		5		6		3		1
6			5		7			2
	3		2	5	6		1	
7								6
	6		9	7	1		3	
3			7		5			9
1		4		2		6		7
		9		1		4		

1	2	3	4	5	6	7	8	9
E	R	V	E	D	O	D	N	A

Clue:
This is the capital of Colorado, which means "colored red" in Spanish. The state was named after the Colorado River, which can look red because it flows through canyons of red stone.

221

Sudoku Extra 103

When you have completed this Sudoku puzzle, use the code box to work out the secret, highlighted word. (You may not need to use all the letters.)

	9	3		2		8	4	
			1		3			
7				5				2
5			9	6	2			4
9		8		4		2		3
6			3	1	8			9
4				9				8
			2		6			
	5	1		7		9	2	

1	2	3	4	5	6	7	8	9
N	R	W	S	E	L	O	F	U

Clue:
This is the state flower of Kansas, where you might see it on the prairies in the hot, sunny summers.

223

Sudoku Extra 104

When you have completed this Sudoku puzzle, use the
code box to work out the secret, highlighted word.
(You may not need to use all the letters.)

	3	1				9	4	
		4	3		7	8		
6			1	4	9			7
3		8		5		7		1
5		6		8		4		2
9			2	1	4			3
		3	5		6	2		
	6	2				1	5	

1	2	3	4	5	6	7	8	9
M	O	A	E	I	T	A	N	N

Clue:
Nicknamed the Treasure State, gold, silver, and
copper were found in its mountains.

Sudoku Extra 105

When you have completed this Sudoku puzzle, use the
code box to work out the secret, highlighted word.
(You may not need to use all the letters.)

4								8
	2	5		4		9	3	
	3	6	2		7	4	1	
			3	2	1			
3	5						7	2
			8	7	5			
	1	3	4		6	7	8	
	7	4		8		2	6	
9								4

1	2	3	4	5	6	7	8	9
S	A	R	A	K	N	B	E	E

Clue:
This state's capital is Lincoln. They grow more
popcorn here than in any other state!

Sudoku Extra 106

When you have completed this Sudoku puzzle, use the code box to work out the secret, highlighted word. (You may not need to use all the letters.)

		1			6		
	6	7	4		5	2	3	
9	3		7		1		4	8
2				1				5
	5						6	
6				4				7
7	1		3		6		2	4
	8	6	1		7	9	5	
		5				7		

1	2	3	4	5	6	7	8	9
G	O	A	R	P	A	N	I	A

Clue:
These famous Falls are in New York. Also in the state of New York are the Adirondack Mountains, the Finger Lakes, and, of course, New York City.

Sudoku Extra 107

When you have completed this Sudoku puzzle, use the code box to work out the secret, highlighted word. (You may not need to use all the letters.)

6		3		2		1		8
	9			4			5	
			7		8			
	8	2	5		4	9	6	
	6						2	
	5	7	8		2	3	1	
			4		6			
	1			5			8	
5		8		7		2		6

1	2	3	4	5	6	7	8	9
N	I	A	A	I	B	D	E	N

Clue:
Known as the "Crossroads of America" because of its central location, its capital is Indianapolis.

Sudoku Extra 108

When you have completed this Sudoku puzzle, use the code box to work out the secret, highlighted word. (You may not need to use all the letters.)

	2		1		6		9	
	1	9		4		8	6	
	8	6				7	2	
		8	3		5	4		
		3				5		
		7	8		9	6		
	7	2				1	5	
	3	4		9		2	8	
	5		6		2		4	

1	2	3	4	5	6	7	8	9
D	I	A	R	N	L	C	E	A

Clue:
This is the state bird of West Virginia, which is also known as the Mountain State. In fact, hills and mountains cover almost all of West Virginia!

Sudoku Extra 109

When you have completed this Sudoku puzzle, use the code box to work out the secret, highlighted word. (You may not need to use all the letters.)

8			1		3			7
3		4				9		1
	6	7		9		2	5	
			8	6	4			
	7			1			6	
			7	3	5			
	3	6		8		4	9	
9		5				7		8
4			9		2			6

1	2	3	4	5	6	7	8	9
P	O	I	A	D	R	W	E	H

Clue:
This state is known as the Gem State. In fact, it produces some of the finest garnets, opals, sapphires, and rubies in the world.

Sudoku Extra 110

When you have completed this Sudoku puzzle, use the
code box to work out the secret, highlighted word.
(You may not need to use all the letters.)

	1		2	6	4		9	
	6	5	7		8	4	1	
	2						7	
8		3		7		1		5
2		6		9		7		4
	3						4	
	4	1	5		7	8	3	
	8		3	4	6		5	

1	2	3	4	5	6	7	8	9
A	R	D	A	F	R	H	T	O

Clue:
This is the capital of Connecticut, also known as
the Constitution State because it was the first
colony in the New World to have its
own constitution.

Sudoku Extra 111

When you have completed this Sudoku puzzle, use the code box to work out the secret, highlighted word. (You may not need to use all the letters.)

	7		6		5		4	
8								1
	6	9		1	3			
	3	2		8	1			
2	1		5		3		7	9
	4	1		6	8			
	5	8		2	7			
9								5
	6		7		9		3	

1	2	3	4	5	6	7	8	9
Z	N	O	I	V	B	R	U	K

Clue:

This friendly bird is the state bird of Michigan. Michigan is surrounded by four of the five Great Lakes and has more lake shoreline than any other state!

239

Sudoku Extra 112

When you have completed this Sudoku puzzle, use the code box to work out the secret, highlighted word. (You may not need to use all the letters.)

	8	4	9	6	5	3	1	
	1						9	
		9	7		3	6		
6				4				1
	4		6		7		3	
8				9				7
		5	1		4	8		
	7						5	
	3	8	5	7	9	2	4	

1	2	3	4	5	6	7	8	9
O	W	I	H	E	I	A	A	P

Clue:
The Aloha State is the only state in the USA that isn't part of the continent of North America.

Sudoku Extra 113

When you have completed this Sudoku puzzle, use the
code box to work out the secret, highlighted word.
(You may not need to use all the letters.)

			3		7			
	8	6	2	4	5	9	7	
3		5				2		4
	9		5	3	2		6	
	5		8	7	1		2	
7		4				6		2
	6	1	4	2	9	5	3	
			7		3			

1	2	3	4	5	6	7	8	9
H	B	O	I	C	O	L	M	H

Clue:
Annie Oakley, the famous sharpshooter, grew up
here, in the Buckeye State.

Sudoku Extra 114

When you have completed this Sudoku puzzle, use the code box to work out the secret, highlighted word. (You may not need to use all the letters.)

		8	1	7	9	2		
	7		8	5	4		9	
4								5
	5		6	9	2		1	
		6				3		
	2		3	8	1		5	
2								1
	6		9	1	5		3	
		9	4	2	6	5		

1	2	3	4	5	6	7	8	9
D	B	N	T	R	N	E	T	O

Clue:
More people live in the state of New Jersey per square mile than in any other state! This is its capital.

Sudoku Extra 115

When you have completed this Sudoku puzzle, use the code box to work out the secret, highlighted word. (You may not need to use all the letters.)

	9	3	4	2	7	8	6	
6	4			1			2	5
3			7	5	4			6
		6				5		
4			2	6	8			7
9	6			4			7	8
	5	1	8	9	6	4	3	

1	2	3	4	5	6	7	8	9
K	W	A	G	I	O	Y	M	N

Clue:
The meadowlark is the official bird of this state, where sheep and cattle outnumber people five to one!

247

Sudoku Extra 116

When you have completed this Sudoku puzzle, use the code box to work out the secret, highlighted word. (You may not need to use all the letters.)

9								1
	4	7		1		2	8	
8			9		2			4
7		9	5		3	8		2
		2				7		
4		3	2		6	1		5
1			8		9			6
	3	8		6		9	5	
6								8

1	2	3	4	5	6	7	8	9
N	A	S	A	M	B	E	O	L

Clue:
This is the capital of Oregon, the destination of thousands of American pioneers who traveled the Oregon Trail.

Sudoku Extra 117

When you have completed this Sudoku puzzle, use the code box to work out the secret, highlighted word. (You may not need to use all the letters.)

	1						5	
	9	5				3	6	
	4	8	9	6	5	2	7	
1			2		4			5
7			8		6			3
	3	6	4	8	7	9	1	
	7	9				6	3	
	2						4	

1	2	3	4	5	6	7	8	9
R	U	A	L	C	E	D	O	G

Clue:
In 1849 many people rushed to California looking for this!

Sudoku Extra 118

When you have completed this Sudoku puzzle, use the code box to work out the secret, highlighted word. (You may not need to use all the letters.)

	9	8	6		3	2	7	
	3		7		2		5	
		2				9		
7	8	9				3	4	5
2	1	4				6	9	7
		7				8		
	4		2		9		1	
	6	5	8		4	7	2	

1	2	3	4	5	6	7	8	9
L	U	Q	M	C	I	A	B	O

Clue:
This is the capital of South Carolina—one of the world's leading peach producers!

253

Sudoku Extra 119

When you have completed this Sudoku puzzle, use the code box to work out the secret, highlighted word. (You may not need to use all the letters.)

				4				
2	9		8		3		6	4
1	4			6			2	7
		6	2	3	1	9		
		9				3		
		1	9	8	6	2		
7	3			5			8	9
9	6		3		8		5	1
				9				

1	2	3	4	5	6	7	8	9
A	I	A	S	U	L	I	O	N

Clue:
You will find the cities of New Orleans and Baton Rouge in this state.

Sudoku Extra 120

When you have completed this Sudoku puzzle, use the
code box to work out the secret, highlighted word.
(You may not need to use all the letters.)

	4						7	
		9	2		4	8		
7		1	9	8	3	5		2
9			4		2			8
		6				9		
8			7		1			3
6		3	5	4	8	2		7
		2	3			7	4	
	8						3	

1	2	3	4	5	6	7	8	9
S	K	V	N	O	A	L	S	E

Clue:
The state of Minnesota has more than fifteen
thousand of these—so many that they ran out of
original names! Can you find out what they are?

Solutions

No. 1

2	3	1	4
4	1	3	2
1	4	2	3
3	2	4	1

No. 2

1	2	3	4
4	3	2	1
2	1	4	3
3	4	1	2

No. 3

1	2	3	4
4	3	1	2
3	4	2	1
2	1	4	3

No. 4

1	2	3	4
3	4	1	2
4	1	2	3
2	3	4	1

No. 5

4	1	3	2
2	3	1	4
3	4	2	1
1	2	4	3

No. 6

2	4	3	1
1	3	2	4
4	2	1	3
3	1	4	2

No. 7

2	3	4	1
4	1	2	3
1	4	3	2
3	2	1	4

No. 8

2	1	4	3
4	3	2	1
3	4	1	2
1	2	3	4

No. 9

1	3	2	4
2	4	1	3
4	2	3	1
3	1	4	2

No. 10

1	2	4	3
4	3	2	1
3	4	1	2
2	1	3	4

No. 11

4	2	1	3
1	3	2	4
3	1	4	2
2	4	3	1

No. 12

1	3	2	4
2	4	3	1
3	1	4	2
4	2	1	3

No. 13

4	1	2	3
2	3	4	1
3	4	1	2
1	2	3	4

No. 14

2	1	3	4
4	3	1	2
1	4	2	3
3	2	4	1

No. 15

4	2	1	3
3	1	2	4
2	3	4	1
1	4	3	2

No. 16

1	4	3	2
3	2	4	1
2	3	1	4
4	1	2	3

No. 17

1	3	2	4
4	2	3	1
3	4	1	2
2	1	4	3

No. 18

3	2	1	4
1	4	2	3
4	1	3	2
2	3	4	1

No. 19

4	3	2	1
1	2	3	4
3	1	4	2
2	4	1	3

No. 20

3	1	4	2
2	4	3	1
4	2	1	3
1	3	2	4

No. 21

4	3	1	5	2	6
2	5	6	1	4	3
5	6	3	2	1	4
1	4	2	6	3	5
3	1	5	4	6	2
6	2	4	3	5	1

No. 22

2	4	5	6	1	3
1	3	6	5	2	4
5	6	1	4	3	2
4	2	3	1	6	5
6	5	2	3	4	1
3	1	4	2	5	6

No. 23

3	5	6	2	1	4
4	2	1	5	6	3
2	3	5	6	4	1
6	1	4	3	2	5
5	4	2	1	3	6
1	6	3	4	5	2

No. 24

6	2	1	4	3	5
3	5	4	6	2	1
4	3	2	1	5	6
5	1	6	2	4	3
2	6	3	5	1	4
1	4	5	3	6	2

No. 25

2	6	5	4	1	3
1	4	3	2	6	5
5	3	2	1	4	6
4	1	6	5	3	2
6	5	1	3	2	4
3	2	4	6	5	1

No. 26

4	3	6	1	2	5
5	2	1	3	6	4
6	1	3	4	5	2
2	5	4	6	3	1
3	4	5	2	1	6
1	6	2	5	4	3

No. 27

4	6	2	5	1	3
5	1	3	4	6	2
1	3	4	2	5	6
2	5	6	3	4	1
3	4	1	6	2	5
6	2	5	1	3	4

No. 28

2	1	4	5	6	3
3	6	5	4	2	1
5	4	6	1	3	2
1	2	3	6	5	4
6	3	1	2	4	5
4	5	2	3	1	6

No. 29

4	5	2	1	6	3
1	3	6	4	5	2
2	6	1	3	4	5
3	4	5	2	1	6
5	1	3	6	2	4
6	2	4	5	3	1

No. 30

6	5	1	4	2	3
2	4	3	5	6	1
3	2	4	6	1	5
1	6	5	3	4	2
5	1	6	2	3	4
4	3	2	1	5	6

No. 31

2	1	5	3	6	4
6	3	4	2	5	1
4	5	1	6	3	2
3	6	2	1	4	5
5	2	3	4	1	6
1	4	6	5	2	3

No. 32

4	1	2	3	5	6
6	3	5	1	2	4
3	5	1	6	4	2
2	4	6	5	3	1
1	2	3	4	6	5
5	6	4	2	1	3

No. 33

3	5	1	6	2	4
4	6	2	3	1	5
5	1	3	4	6	2
2	4	6	5	3	1
6	2	5	1	4	3
1	3	4	2	5	6

No. 34

5	3	2	1	6	4
6	1	4	3	2	5
4	2	1	6	5	3
3	6	5	4	1	2
1	5	3	2	4	6
2	4	6	5	3	1

No. 35

4	5	6	1	2	3
3	1	2	6	4	5
6	2	4	3	5	1
1	3	5	4	6	2
5	4	1	2	3	6
2	6	3	5	1	4

No. 36

4	3	1	6	2	5
2	5	6	4	1	3
1	2	4	3	5	6
5	6	3	1	4	2
3	1	2	5	6	4
6	4	5	2	3	1

No. 37

2	3	1	5	4	6
4	5	6	2	1	3
6	2	4	3	5	1
3	1	5	4	6	2
5	6	2	1	3	4
1	4	3	6	2	5

No. 38

6	2	5	1	4	3
3	4	1	6	5	2
4	5	3	2	6	1
1	6	2	4	3	5
5	1	4	3	2	6
2	3	6	5	1	4

No. 39

2	4	5	1	3	6
1	3	6	2	5	4
3	2	1	6	4	5
5	6	4	3	1	2
4	1	2	5	6	3
6	5	3	4	2	1

No. 40

6	3	5	2	1	4
4	1	2	5	6	3
1	2	4	6	3	5
5	6	3	1	4	2
3	5	1	4	2	6
2	4	6	3	5	1

No. 41

2	1	4	5	3	6
5	6	3	1	4	2
3	5	6	2	1	4
4	2	1	3	6	5
1	4	2	6	5	3
6	3	5	4	2	1

No. 42

6	5	2	4	3	1
4	3	1	2	5	6
1	4	5	6	2	3
2	6	3	5	1	4
5	1	4	3	6	2
3	2	6	1	4	5

No. 43

2	5	3	6	1	4
4	6	1	2	5	3
6	1	4	3	2	5
3	2	5	4	6	1
1	3	2	5	4	6
5	4	6	1	3	2

No. 44

1	5	6	3	4	2
2	3	4	5	1	6
5	1	3	6	2	4
4	6	2	1	5	3
3	2	5	4	6	1
6	4	1	2	3	5

No. 45

5	4	6	1	2	3
2	3	1	6	4	5
6	1	5	4	3	2
4	2	3	5	6	1
3	5	4	2	1	6
1	6	2	3	5	4

No. 46

3	4	6	1	2	5
5	2	1	3	4	6
4	5	2	6	1	3
1	6	3	4	5	2
6	1	5	2	3	4
2	3	4	5	6	1

No. 47

1	3	4	2	6	5
2	5	6	4	3	1
5	4	1	6	2	3
6	2	3	5	1	4
3	6	5	1	4	2
4	1	2	3	5	6

No. 48

3	4	2	5	1	6
1	6	5	3	2	4
6	5	3	1	4	2
4	2	1	6	5	3
5	3	4	2	6	1
2	1	6	4	3	5

No. 49

3	5	4	2	6	1
6	2	1	3	5	4
4	1	5	6	2	3
2	3	6	1	4	5
5	6	3	4	1	2
1	4	2	5	3	6

No. 50

1	6	5	4	3	2
3	4	2	1	5	6
6	1	3	5	2	4
2	5	4	3	6	1
5	2	1	6	4	3
4	3	6	2	1	5

No. 51

2	6	5	1	3	4
3	1	4	2	5	6
6	5	3	4	2	1
1	4	2	3	6	5
5	3	1	6	4	2
4	2	6	5	1	3

No. 52

6	5	2	3	1	4
1	4	3	6	2	5
5	6	1	4	3	2
3	2	4	5	6	1
2	3	5	1	4	6
4	1	6	2	5	3

No. 53

2	6	4	3	5	1
1	3	5	2	4	6
4	5	1	6	2	3
6	2	3	4	1	5
5	4	6	1	3	2
3	1	2	5	6	4

No. 54

5	6	4	2	3	1
1	3	2	5	6	4
6	2	3	1	4	5
4	1	5	3	2	6
3	4	1	6	5	2
2	5	6	4	1	3

No. 55

3	1	2	6	5	4
5	6	4	3	1	2
2	4	1	5	3	6
6	5	3	4	2	1
4	2	5	1	6	3
1	3	6	2	4	5

No. 56

4	3	5	2	1	6
1	6	2	4	3	5
6	1	4	3	5	2
2	5	3	1	6	4
3	4	6	5	2	1
5	2	1	6	4	3

No. 57

5	6	1	4	2	3
2	4	3	1	6	5
6	1	2	3	5	4
4	3	5	6	1	2
3	5	6	2	4	1
1	2	4	5	3	6

No. 58

2	4	6	1	5	3
5	1	3	2	4	6
1	5	2	6	3	4
6	3	4	5	1	2
3	2	1	4	6	5
4	6	5	3	2	1

No. 59

2	3	1	6	4	5
4	5	6	3	2	1
3	2	4	1	5	6
1	6	5	2	3	4
5	1	2	4	6	3
6	4	3	5	1	2

No. 60

3	2	4	1	6	5
6	5	1	3	4	2
5	6	3	2	1	4
4	1	2	5	3	6
1	4	5	6	2	3
2	3	6	4	5	1

No. 61

5	6	9	7	8	3	4	1	2
4	7	2	1	6	9	3	5	8
1	3	8	5	2	4	9	7	6
8	2	3	4	7	6	1	9	5
9	1	7	8	5	2	6	3	4
6	4	5	9	3	1	8	2	7
7	9	4	6	1	5	2	8	3
2	5	6	3	9	8	7	4	1
3	8	1	2	4	7	5	6	9

No. 62

1	3	9	2	8	5	7	6	4
7	6	5	1	4	9	8	3	2
2	8	4	6	7	3	9	1	5
5	7	8	3	9	1	4	2	6
4	2	6	7	5	8	3	9	1
3	9	1	4	2	6	5	8	7
8	5	7	9	1	2	6	4	3
6	4	2	8	3	7	1	5	9
9	1	3	5	6	4	2	7	8

No. 63

4	8	2	5	9	3	1	7	6
3	5	6	8	1	7	4	2	9
9	1	7	2	4	6	3	8	5
7	9	4	6	3	1	8	5	2
2	3	5	4	7	8	6	9	1
1	6	8	9	5	2	7	3	4
8	4	9	7	6	5	2	1	3
5	2	3	1	8	4	9	6	7
6	7	1	3	2	9	5	4	8

No. 64

9	1	7	4	8	2	6	3	5
8	5	6	1	3	7	9	4	2
3	2	4	5	6	9	8	7	1
6	8	9	3	5	4	1	2	7
1	3	2	7	9	8	4	5	6
7	4	5	2	1	6	3	8	9
4	9	8	6	7	5	2	1	3
2	7	1	9	4	3	5	6	8
5	6	3	8	2	1	7	9	4

No. 65

3	4	5	7	2	8	9	6	1
6	8	2	1	4	9	3	7	5
9	7	1	5	3	6	4	8	2
1	3	4	2	9	7	6	5	8
2	6	8	4	5	3	1	9	7
7	5	9	6	8	1	2	3	4
4	9	3	8	7	2	5	1	6
5	1	7	9	6	4	8	2	3
8	2	6	3	1	5	7	4	9

No. 66

6	7	1	2	9	8	5	3	4
3	2	4	1	5	7	6	8	9
8	9	5	3	6	4	7	1	2
1	6	2	7	4	5	8	9	3
5	3	8	9	2	1	4	7	6
7	4	9	8	3	6	1	2	5
4	1	3	5	8	2	9	6	7
9	8	6	4	7	3	2	5	1
2	5	7	6	1	9	3	4	8

No. 67

7	2	6	1	3	5	9	8	4
4	9	1	7	8	6	3	2	5
8	3	5	9	2	4	6	7	1
2	7	3	4	5	1	8	9	6
6	8	4	2	7	9	1	5	3
1	5	9	3	6	8	2	4	7
5	6	2	8	1	7	4	3	9
3	4	7	6	9	2	5	1	8
9	1	8	5	4	3	7	6	2

No. 68

5	2	8	4	9	3	6	1	7
1	9	7	6	8	2	5	4	3
4	6	3	5	1	7	9	2	8
9	5	4	8	7	6	2	3	1
3	7	2	1	4	5	8	6	9
8	1	6	3	2	9	7	5	4
6	4	5	9	3	8	1	7	2
7	3	9	2	5	1	4	8	6
2	8	1	7	6	4	3	9	5

No. 69

5	9	2	6	8	1	4	7	3
1	8	3	9	7	4	5	6	2
6	7	4	5	3	2	8	9	1
2	6	7	4	9	8	1	3	5
3	5	1	7	2	6	9	4	8
8	4	9	3	1	5	6	2	7
7	1	6	2	5	9	3	8	4
4	3	8	1	6	7	2	5	9
9	2	5	8	4	3	7	1	6

No. 70

3	2	6	7	1	8	9	4	5
5	7	9	6	2	4	1	8	3
8	1	4	3	9	5	2	7	6
2	8	1	9	5	7	6	3	4
4	3	7	1	6	2	5	9	8
6	9	5	4	8	3	7	2	1
7	4	2	5	3	6	8	1	9
9	6	3	8	7	1	4	5	2
1	5	8	2	4	9	3	6	7

No. 71

9	4	8	3	1	5	7	2	6
1	5	7	6	2	9	4	3	8
6	2	3	4	8	7	1	5	9
3	8	5	9	6	4	2	7	1
2	1	4	7	3	8	6	9	5
7	6	9	2	5	1	8	4	3
8	9	2	5	4	6	3	1	7
4	7	6	1	9	3	5	8	2
5	3	1	8	7	2	9	6	4

No. 72

8	1	2	9	6	7	5	3	4
4	5	7	8	3	2	1	9	6
6	9	3	4	5	1	7	2	8
1	7	9	5	8	6	2	4	3
3	4	8	2	1	9	6	5	7
5	2	6	7	4	3	9	8	1
9	3	1	6	2	4	8	7	5
2	6	5	3	7	8	4	1	9
7	8	4	1	9	5	3	6	2

No. 73

1	3	5	2	6	4	8	7	9
7	2	4	8	9	3	5	1	6
9	8	6	5	7	1	3	4	2
6	4	1	3	8	7	2	9	5
5	7	2	6	4	9	1	3	8
3	9	8	1	2	5	7	6	4
2	5	7	4	1	6	9	8	3
4	1	3	9	5	8	6	2	7
8	6	9	7	3	2	4	5	1

No. 74

6	8	7	4	3	5	9	1	2
1	3	9	7	2	6	4	8	5
2	4	5	1	9	8	7	3	6
7	5	2	6	4	1	3	9	8
8	9	4	2	7	3	5	6	1
3	1	6	8	5	9	2	4	7
4	6	3	5	1	2	8	7	9
9	2	8	3	6	7	1	5	4
5	7	1	9	8	4	6	2	3

No. 75

6	2	5	1	3	4	9	7	8
3	9	8	5	7	2	4	6	1
1	7	4	8	6	9	5	3	2
7	6	3	4	1	8	2	9	5
5	4	2	3	9	7	8	1	6
9	8	1	2	5	6	7	4	3
8	1	7	9	2	3	6	5	4
2	5	6	7	4	1	3	8	9
4	3	9	6	8	5	1	2	7

No. 76

4	9	6	8	7	3	5	2	1
5	7	8	9	1	2	6	3	4
2	1	3	5	4	6	9	7	8
7	2	5	3	6	4	8	1	9
3	8	1	7	5	9	4	6	2
6	4	9	2	8	1	3	5	7
1	5	7	6	9	8	2	4	3
9	3	4	1	2	5	7	8	6
8	6	2	4	3	7	1	9	5

No. 77

2	6	9	7	1	5	3	8	4
8	1	5	3	2	4	7	6	9
7	3	4	6	9	8	5	1	2
5	9	2	8	7	3	6	4	1
6	7	1	5	4	2	9	3	8
4	8	3	1	6	9	2	7	5
3	5	7	2	8	1	4	9	6
1	4	6	9	5	7	8	2	3
9	2	8	4	3	6	1	5	7

No. 78

8	9	7	5	3	6	4	1	2
2	3	1	4	8	9	5	7	6
6	5	4	7	2	1	9	3	8
9	8	5	3	4	2	1	6	7
4	1	3	6	7	5	8	2	9
7	6	2	9	1	8	3	4	5
1	4	6	8	5	7	2	9	3
5	2	9	1	6	3	7	8	4
3	7	8	2	9	4	6	5	1

No. 79

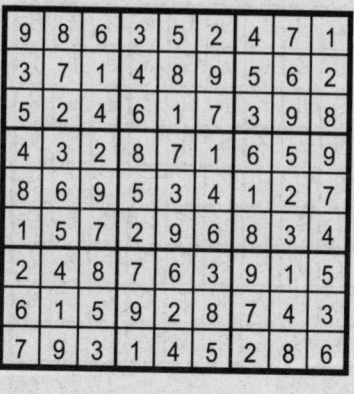

9	8	6	3	5	2	4	7	1
3	7	1	4	8	9	5	6	2
5	2	4	6	1	7	3	9	8
4	3	2	8	7	1	6	5	9
8	6	9	5	3	4	1	2	7
1	5	7	2	9	6	8	3	4
2	4	8	7	6	3	9	1	5
6	1	5	9	2	8	7	4	3
7	9	3	1	4	5	2	8	6

No. 80

6	3	2	5	8	1	7	4	9
5	7	9	6	4	3	2	8	1
1	4	8	2	9	7	6	3	5
8	6	1	7	5	2	4	9	3
3	5	4	9	6	8	1	2	7
9	2	7	3	1	4	8	5	6
2	1	6	8	3	5	9	7	4
7	9	3	4	2	6	5	1	8
4	8	5	1	7	9	3	6	2

No. 81

8	2	7	4	6	1	5	3	9
6	5	9	8	7	3	1	2	4
4	1	3	5	2	9	8	6	7
1	6	8	3	4	5	7	9	2
3	7	4	1	9	2	6	5	8
5	9	2	7	8	6	3	4	1
7	8	6	9	3	4	2	1	5
2	4	5	6	1	8	9	7	3
9	3	1	2	5	7	4	8	6

No. 82

7	6	9	4	8	1	3	5	2
3	4	2	6	9	5	8	7	1
5	1	8	7	2	3	9	4	6
8	7	3	2	5	9	1	6	4
9	5	6	1	4	8	7	2	3
1	2	4	3	7	6	5	9	8
6	9	7	8	1	2	4	3	5
4	3	1	5	6	7	2	8	9
2	8	5	9	3	4	6	1	7

No. 83

5	9	4	3	8	1	7	2	6
1	8	7	4	6	2	3	9	5
2	3	6	9	5	7	4	8	1
8	6	3	2	7	4	1	5	9
4	2	5	1	9	6	8	3	7
7	1	9	8	3	5	2	6	4
3	5	2	7	4	9	6	1	8
6	7	1	5	2	8	9	4	3
9	4	8	6	1	3	5	7	2

No. 84

6	4	9	7	8	1	5	3	2
3	2	8	4	5	6	7	9	1
1	5	7	2	9	3	6	4	8
4	1	5	9	2	8	3	6	7
8	3	6	1	4	7	2	5	9
9	7	2	6	3	5	8	1	4
5	9	3	8	1	2	4	7	6
2	6	1	5	7	4	9	8	3
7	8	4	3	6	9	1	2	5

No. 85

8	4	9	7	6	5	2	3	1
2	3	1	9	4	8	6	7	5
6	7	5	1	2	3	8	9	4
1	2	3	4	7	6	5	8	9
5	9	7	8	3	2	4	1	6
4	6	8	5	9	1	3	2	7
3	5	2	6	1	9	7	4	8
9	8	4	2	5	7	1	6	3
7	1	6	3	8	4	9	5	2

No. 86

5	6	7	4	9	3	2	1	8
9	8	2	7	1	6	3	4	5
1	3	4	8	5	2	9	7	6
7	9	8	2	6	5	4	3	1
6	1	5	3	4	9	8	2	7
4	2	3	1	7	8	6	5	9
3	5	9	6	2	1	7	8	4
8	4	1	9	3	7	5	6	2
2	7	6	5	8	4	1	9	3

No. 87

4	7	2	3	5	1	6	8	9
8	6	9	2	7	4	1	3	5
3	1	5	6	9	8	4	7	2
2	9	1	8	6	5	7	4	3
6	4	3	7	1	9	5	2	8
7	5	8	4	3	2	9	6	1
1	8	7	9	2	6	3	5	4
5	3	4	1	8	7	2	9	6
9	2	6	5	4	3	8	1	7

No. 88

2	4	7	8	5	3	9	6	1
9	1	8	2	6	4	3	5	7
6	3	5	9	7	1	4	2	8
8	9	6	5	4	7	2	1	3
5	2	1	3	8	9	7	4	6
3	7	4	1	2	6	5	8	9
4	8	3	7	1	2	6	9	5
1	6	9	4	3	5	8	7	2
7	5	2	6	9	8	1	3	4

No. 89

6	1	7	8	5	4	2	3	9
8	2	9	6	7	3	1	5	4
4	3	5	2	1	9	6	8	7
5	4	3	9	2	8	7	1	6
1	9	2	7	6	5	3	4	8
7	8	6	3	4	1	9	2	5
3	6	8	5	9	2	4	7	1
2	7	1	4	8	6	5	9	3
9	5	4	1	3	7	8	6	2

No. 90

3	6	8	5	1	4	9	7	2
1	2	5	9	7	6	4	8	3
9	4	7	2	3	8	5	6	1
6	8	9	1	5	3	2	4	7
4	5	2	8	9	7	3	1	6
7	1	3	4	6	2	8	5	9
2	3	4	7	8	1	6	9	5
5	7	6	3	4	9	1	2	8
8	9	1	6	2	5	7	3	4

Extra 91

4	3	6	2	1	5
2	1	5	4	3	6
5	4	2	1	6	3
3	6	1	5	2	4
6	2	4	3	5	1
1	5	3	6	4	2

Extra 92

4	2	6	1	3	5
1	5	3	4	6	2
6	3	2	5	4	1
5	4	1	3	2	6
2	1	4	6	5	3
3	6	5	2	1	4

Extra 93

3	1	6	2	5	4
5	2	4	3	1	6
6	5	2	1	4	3
4	3	1	5	6	2
1	6	3	4	2	5
2	4	5	6	3	1

Extra 94

3	5	6	2	4	1
2	4	1	5	3	6
4	3	5	6	1	2
6	1	2	4	5	3
1	2	4	3	6	5
5	6	3	1	2	4

Extra 95

4	6	3	1	5	2
2	1	5	4	6	3
5	2	6	3	1	4
3	4	1	6	2	5
6	5	4	2	3	1
1	3	2	5	4	6

HIDDEN WORDS:

Extra 91: MAINE
Extra 92: IOWA
Extra 93: UTAH
Extra 94: NEVADA
Extra 95: TEXAS

Extra 96

5	9	7	8	4	6	3	2	1
6	3	2	1	9	5	8	4	7
8	1	4	3	2	7	9	5	6
7	2	1	6	5	9	4	3	8
3	4	5	2	1	8	6	7	9
9	8	6	4	7	3	5	1	2
4	7	9	5	6	1	2	8	3
2	6	8	7	3	4	1	9	5
1	5	3	9	8	2	7	6	4

Extra 97

9	1	7	8	5	2	3	6	4
6	4	5	3	1	7	8	2	9
8	2	3	4	9	6	1	7	5
7	3	4	5	2	8	9	1	6
5	6	9	1	7	4	2	3	8
2	8	1	9	6	3	5	4	7
1	7	2	6	8	9	4	5	3
3	5	8	7	4	1	6	9	2
4	9	6	2	3	5	7	8	1

Extra 98

9	6	1	3	7	4	2	5	8
4	2	8	6	5	9	3	1	7
3	7	5	1	2	8	4	9	6
6	9	3	2	8	7	1	4	5
7	8	2	4	1	5	6	3	9
1	5	4	9	3	6	8	7	2
8	3	9	5	4	2	7	6	1
2	4	6	7	9	1	5	8	3
5	1	7	8	6	3	9	2	4

Extra 99

7	8	1	5	3	2	6	4	9
4	9	6	8	1	7	5	3	2
3	2	5	6	9	4	7	8	1
5	6	2	1	8	3	9	7	4
9	4	3	7	6	5	1	2	8
1	7	8	4	2	9	3	5	6
8	5	7	9	4	6	2	1	3
2	1	9	3	7	8	4	6	5
6	3	4	2	5	1	8	9	7

Extra 100

3	4	1	2	7	5	9	8	6
5	7	8	6	9	3	2	4	1
2	9	6	8	4	1	5	7	3
9	3	7	4	5	8	6	1	2
8	1	2	9	3	6	4	5	7
6	5	4	7	1	2	3	9	8
1	6	3	5	8	9	7	2	4
7	2	5	1	6	4	8	3	9
4	8	9	3	2	7	1	6	5

HIDDEN WORDS:

Extra 96: MISSOURI
Extra 97: GEORGIA
Extra 98: OLYMPIA
Extra 99: DELAWARE
Extra 100: CHICKADEE

Extra 101

9	1	4	5	3	2	6	8	7
3	5	6	7	4	8	2	1	9
8	7	2	1	9	6	4	3	5
5	6	9	3	2	4	1	7	8
4	2	7	9	8	1	5	6	3
1	8	3	6	5	7	9	2	4
7	4	8	2	6	5	3	9	1
6	3	1	4	7	9	8	5	2
2	9	5	8	1	3	7	4	6

Extra 102

2	4	7	1	9	3	8	6	5
8	9	5	4	6	2	3	7	1
6	1	3	5	8	7	9	4	2
9	3	8	2	5	6	7	1	4
7	5	1	8	3	4	2	9	6
4	6	2	9	7	1	5	3	8
3	2	6	7	4	5	1	8	9
1	8	4	3	2	9	6	5	7
5	7	9	6	1	8	4	2	3

Extra 103

1	9	3	6	2	7	8	4	5
2	4	5	1	8	3	6	9	7
7	8	6	4	5	9	3	1	2
5	3	7	9	6	2	1	8	4
9	1	8	7	4	5	2	6	3
6	2	4	3	1	8	5	7	9
4	6	2	5	9	1	7	3	8
8	7	9	2	3	6	4	5	1
3	5	1	8	7	4	9	2	6

Extra 104

7	3	1	8	2	5	9	4	6
2	9	4	3	6	7	8	1	5
6	8	5	1	4	9	3	2	7
3	4	8	6	5	2	7	9	1
1	2	9	4	7	3	5	6	8
5	7	6	9	8	1	4	3	2
9	5	7	2	1	4	6	8	3
8	1	3	5	9	6	2	7	4
4	6	2	7	3	8	1	5	9

Extra 105

4	9	7	5	1	3	6	2	8
1	2	5	6	4	8	9	3	7
8	3	6	2	9	7	4	1	5
7	8	9	3	2	1	5	4	6
3	5	1	9	6	4	8	7	2
6	4	2	8	7	5	3	9	1
2	1	3	4	5	6	7	8	9
5	7	4	1	8	9	2	6	3
9	6	8	7	3	2	1	5	4

HIDDEN WORDS:

Extra 101: FLORIDA
Extra 102: DENVER
Extra 103: SUNFLOWER
Extra 104: MONTANA
Extra 105: NEBRASKA

Extra 106

5	4	1	2	3	8	6	7	9
8	6	7	4	9	5	2	3	1
9	3	2	7	6	1	5	4	8
2	7	8	6	1	3	4	9	5
1	5	4	8	7	9	3	6	2
6	9	3	5	4	2	1	8	7
7	1	9	3	5	6	8	2	4
4	8	6	1	2	7	9	5	3
3	2	5	9	8	4	7	1	6

Extra 107

6	7	3	9	2	5	1	4	8
8	9	1	6	4	3	7	5	2
4	2	5	7	1	8	6	3	9
1	8	2	5	3	4	9	6	7
3	6	4	1	9	7	8	2	5
9	5	7	8	6	2	3	1	4
2	3	9	4	8	6	5	7	1
7	1	6	2	5	9	4	8	3
5	4	8	3	7	1	2	9	6

Extra 108

7	2	5	1	8	6	3	9	4
3	1	9	2	4	7	8	6	5
4	8	6	9	5	3	7	2	1
1	6	8	3	2	5	4	7	9
2	9	3	7	6	4	5	1	8
5	4	7	8	1	9	6	3	2
9	7	2	4	3	8	1	5	6
6	3	4	5	9	1	2	8	7
8	5	1	6	7	2	9	4	3

Extra 109

8	9	2	1	5	3	6	4	7
3	5	4	6	2	7	9	8	1
1	6	7	4	9	8	2	5	3
2	1	9	8	6	4	3	7	5
5	7	3	2	1	9	8	6	4
6	4	8	7	3	5	1	2	9
7	3	6	5	8	1	4	9	2
9	2	5	3	4	6	7	1	8
4	8	1	9	7	2	5	3	6

Extra 110

3	1	7	2	6	4	5	9	8
9	6	5	7	3	8	4	1	2
4	2	8	9	5	1	3	7	6
8	9	3	4	7	2	1	6	5
1	7	4	6	8	5	9	2	3
2	5	6	1	9	3	7	8	4
5	3	2	8	1	9	6	4	7
6	4	1	5	2	7	8	3	9
7	8	9	3	4	6	2	5	1

HIDDEN WORDS:

Extra 106: NIAGARA
Extra 107: INDIANA
Extra 108: CARDINAL
Extra 109: IDAHO
Extra 110: HARTFORD

Extra 111

3	7	1	6	8	5	9	4	2
8	2	9	4	3	7	5	6	1
5	4	6	9	2	1	3	8	7
6	9	3	2	7	8	1	5	4
2	1	8	5	4	3	6	7	9
7	5	4	1	9	6	8	2	3
4	3	5	8	1	2	7	9	6
9	8	7	3	6	4	2	1	5
1	6	2	7	5	9	4	3	8

Extra 112

7	8	4	9	6	5	3	1	2
3	1	6	4	8	2	7	9	5
5	2	9	7	1	3	6	8	4
6	9	7	3	4	8	5	2	1
2	4	1	6	5	7	9	3	8
8	5	3	2	9	1	4	6	7
9	6	5	1	2	4	8	7	3
4	7	2	8	3	6	1	5	9
1	3	8	5	7	9	2	4	6

Extra 113

9	4	2	3	1	7	8	5	6
1	8	6	2	4	5	9	7	3
3	7	5	9	8	6	2	1	4
4	9	8	5	3	2	7	6	1
2	1	7	6	9	4	3	8	5
6	5	3	8	7	1	4	2	9
7	3	4	1	5	8	6	9	2
8	6	1	4	2	9	5	3	7
5	2	9	7	6	3	1	4	8

Extra 114

5	3	8	1	7	9	2	4	6
6	7	2	8	5	4	1	9	3
4	9	1	2	6	3	7	8	5
7	5	3	6	9	2	8	1	4
1	8	6	5	4	7	3	2	9
9	2	4	3	8	1	6	5	7
2	4	5	7	3	8	9	6	1
8	6	7	9	1	5	4	3	2
3	1	9	4	2	6	5	7	8

Extra 115

1	2	7	6	8	5	9	4	3
5	9	3	4	2	7	8	6	1
6	4	8	3	1	9	7	2	5
3	8	9	7	5	4	2	1	6
2	7	6	9	3	1	5	8	4
4	1	5	2	6	8	3	9	7
9	6	2	5	4	3	1	7	8
7	5	1	8	9	6	4	3	2
8	3	4	1	7	2	6	5	9

HIDDEN WORDS:

Extra 111: ROBIN
Extra 112: HAWAII
Extra 113: OHIO
Extra 114: TRENTON
Extra 115: WYOMING

Extra 116

9	2	6	7	8	4	5	3	1
3	4	7	6	1	5	2	8	9
8	5	1	9	3	2	6	7	4
7	1	9	5	4	3	8	6	2
5	6	2	1	9	8	7	4	3
4	8	3	2	7	6	1	9	5
1	7	4	8	5	9	3	2	6
2	3	8	4	6	1	9	5	7
6	9	5	3	2	7	4	1	8

Extra 117

6	1	7	3	4	2	8	5	9
2	9	5	1	7	8	3	6	4
3	4	8	9	6	5	2	7	1
1	6	3	2	9	4	7	8	5
9	8	4	7	5	3	1	2	6
7	5	2	8	1	6	4	9	3
5	3	6	4	8	7	9	1	2
4	7	9	5	2	1	6	3	8
8	2	1	6	3	9	5	4	7

Extra 118

4	9	8	6	5	3	2	7	1
6	3	1	7	9	2	4	5	8
5	7	2	4	1	8	9	6	3
7	8	9	1	2	6	3	4	5
3	5	6	9	4	7	1	8	2
2	1	4	3	8	5	6	9	7
9	2	7	5	6	1	8	3	4
8	4	3	2	7	9	5	1	6
1	6	5	8	3	4	7	2	9

Extra 119

6	8	5	7	4	2	1	9	3
2	9	7	8	1	3	5	6	4
1	4	3	5	6	9	8	2	7
4	5	6	2	3	1	9	7	8
8	2	9	4	7	5	3	1	6
3	7	1	9	8	6	2	4	5
7	3	2	1	5	4	6	8	9
9	6	4	3	2	8	7	5	1
5	1	8	6	9	7	4	3	2

Extra 120

2	4	8	1	5	6	3	7	9
3	5	9	2	7	4	8	6	1
7	6	1	9	8	3	5	4	2
9	3	5	4	6	2	7	1	8
1	7	6	8	3	5	9	2	4
8	2	4	7	9	1	6	5	3
6	1	3	5	4	8	2	9	7
5	9	2	3	1	7	4	8	6
4	8	7	6	2	9	1	3	5

HIDDEN WORDS:

Extra 116: SALEM
Extra 117: GOLD
Extra 118: COLUMBIA
Extra 119: LOUISIANA
Extra 120: LAKES

About the Authors

Lindsay Small has been creating puzzles, coloring pages, and other fun and educational printables for children since 2000. Visit her website www.ActivityVillage.co.uk for a huge collection of fun activities and crafts for kids.

Lindsay's family recently caught the Sudoku bug, and, recognizing the potential of Sudoku puzzles for children but finding few puzzles available that were suitable, she decided to make her own. Having a very clever brother to create a Sudoku-generating computer program helped!

Lindsay's first book, *Superstar Sudoku for Kids*, is also published by Price Stern Sloan.

Robin Hammond has always been very clever with his computer and was writing his first programs (for the very first personal computers) when he was fourteen. When Lindsay asked him if he would write a program to generate graded Sudoku puzzles suitable for children, he said no. Luckily he changed his mind!

And he wrote a very good program. Robin has made it possible to grade the Sudoku puzzles in this book very carefully so that they start easy and get gradually more and more difficult. That means that you can improve your Sudoku skills over time and not get discouraged by trying a very difficult puzzle too early on.